Letters to Kenna

Rene Brock

Illustrations by
Lisa Pavlak

Copyright © 2024 by Rene Brock

All rights reserved. This book, or any portion thereof, may not be reproduced in print or digital formats or used in any manner whatsoever without the express written permission of the publisher or author except for the use of brief quotations in a website, book review, or scholarly journal.

First Publication: 2024
ISBN: 9798320895567

This book is dedicated to all children
who need some inspiration, hope, and kindness.

Eight-year-old Rosie sat in her third grade classroom with her eyes glued to the clock. All she wanted was to leave school and find a safe place.

She felt frustrated that her classmates had been so mean to her. Every day Rosie would feel left out and embarrassed because no one would talk to her.

Finally, the dismissal bell rang and Rosie jumped out of her seat as quick as a lightning bolt.

She couldn't wait to go home and sit in her favorite spot under the tree in her backyard.

But on the way home, a terrible rainstorm started pouring down. Rosie started running and her heart was pumping so hard that she thought it was going to jump right out of her chest! Rosie had a million thoughts racing through her head.

Rosie ran straight to her favorite spot under the tree and leaned against the trunk.

She began to sob.

Rosie didn't notice a little caterpillar squirming along her backpack.

As Rosie gazed down at her sneaker, she spotted a small, fuzzy green and yellow caterpillar.

As she blinked, a tear rolled down her cheek and it landed right on top of the caterpillar.

The caterpillar crawled up onto her knee and said, "Hi, my name is Kindra. What's your name?"

"Whoa! You can talk? I never knew that caterpillars could speak! My name is Rosie."

"Why are you crying, Rosie?" Kindra asked.

"I feel so lonely. It has been an awful day," replied Rosie.

Kindra said, "I'm sorry you feel so lonely. We all cry sometimes. Just take a deep breath and try to relax."

Rosie giggled and said, "You are so cute and fuzzy! It would be great to have a friend like you."

Kindra replied, "I would love to be your friend."

Rosie and Kindra went on a long walk through the woods and shared stories about their lives.

It started to get late and
Rosie began to feel tired.

"I better go home and get some rest
before school tomorrow," Rosie said.

Kindra replied, "Get a good night's sleep
and we can meet tomorrow."

Rosie agreed saying, "Yes, let's meet back
at my favorite tree."

"Perfect! I can't wait to see you
tomorrow," Kindra said.

"Look at the view."

"Wow!"

On the first day, Rosie climbed a tree and held Kindra in her right hand. They went all the way to the top, and looked down.

Kindra said, "Wow, what a marvelous view! I bet this is what eagles see from up here! It's amazing to see things from a different perspective. You can always find beauty wherever you go."

Kindra and Rosie played for three straight days. It seemed like they had known each other for a lifetime.

The next day, Kindra and Rosie played hide and seek along the cool, stream. Rosie hid behind a tree, but Kindra could not find her.

Finally, Rosie showed herself and said, "Here I am!"
She laughed. "This is so much fun!"
Kindra replied, "It's always fun to spend time with your friends."

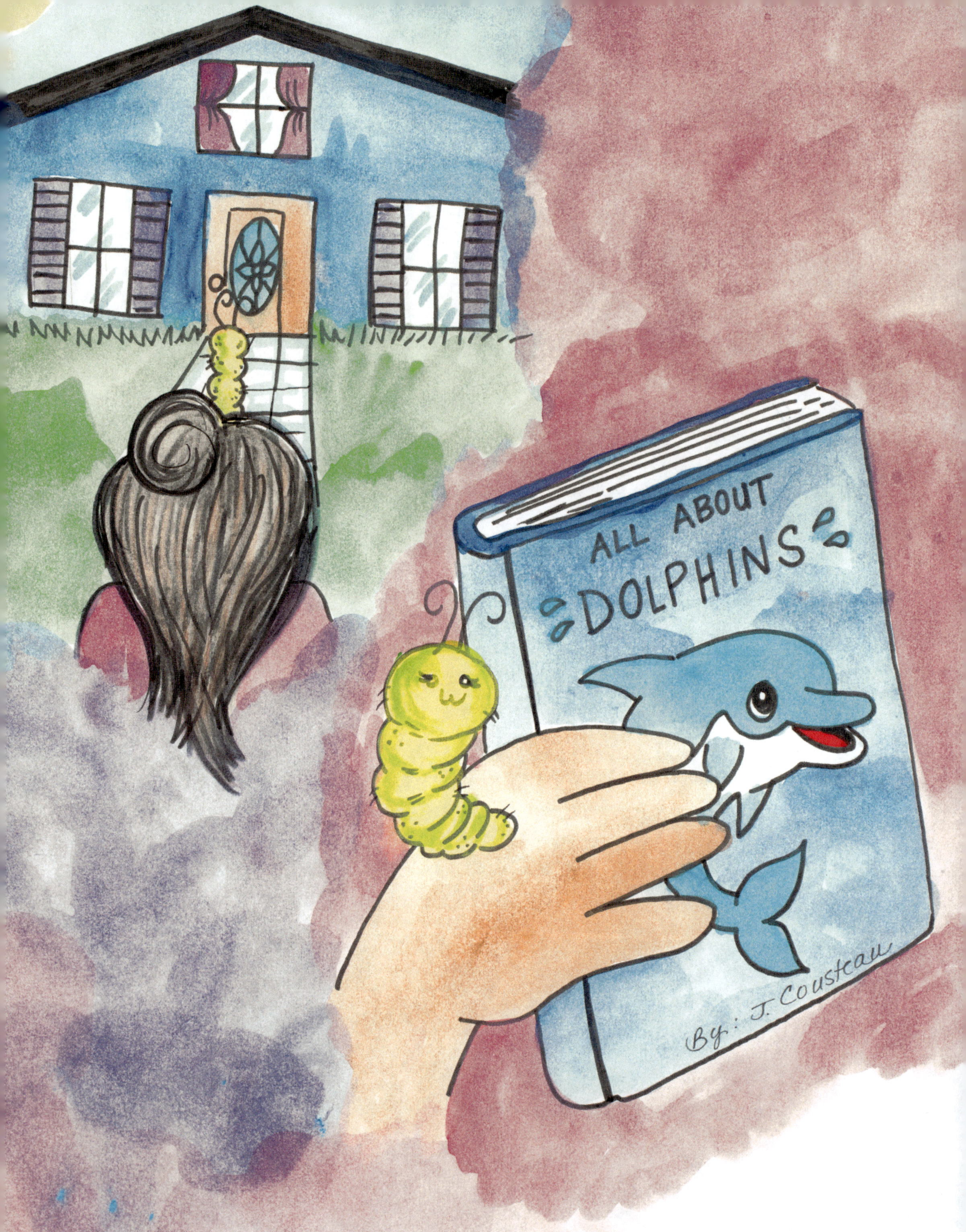
ALL ABOUT
DOLPHINS
By: J. Cousteau

The following morning, Kindra asked, "what should we do today?"

Rosie said, "Let's go to my house so you can see where I live."

When they got to the house, Rosie brought Kindra into her bedroom. Kindra immediately noticed all the different books on her shelves.

Rosie said, "This one is my favorite book!" She pulled out *All About Dolphins* from the shelf. Rosie began reading to Kindra.

Kindra said, "Every time you pick up a book, you get the chance to learn something new. There's so much to explore and discover in the world."

As night fell, they stopped reading and went outside to gaze at the stars and look up at the glowing moon. At that moment, Rosie had an idea.

"Hey Kindra, let's build a campfire and roast some marshmallows."

Kindra replied, "That's a great idea. I would love a fireside snack."

As the flames licked the air, Kindra wrapped herself around Rosie's finger and gave her a caterpillar hug.

Rosie smiled and said, "Kindra, I feel so happy. You are kind and I feel so loved."

18

Kindra replied, "Rosie, always remember that kindness counts. When you show kindness to others, it makes them feel loved."

Rosie listened to her wise friend. The warmth from the fire made her feel sleepy.

Kindra whispered, "It is important to take time to rest and relax."

Rosie replied, "Thank you, Kindra. You are such a good friend."

The next morning Kindra crawled up onto Rosie's shoulder and whispered, "Rosie, I have to go away for a little while. It is time for me to rest in my chrysalis."

Rosie started feeling sad all over again. She became nervous and a large teardrop rolled down her cheek.

"Don't be sad, Rosie. I have an idea! I saw the pen and notebook in your bookbag. We can write letters to each other," Kindra said.

"Here is your notebook. We can use this to write letters back and forth to each other."

Rosie answered, "I will miss you so much, but I will definitely write to you! When you receive my letters, will you write back as soon as you can?"

Kindra replied, "Yes, I promise."

Rosie was disappointed that Kindra had to go away for a while. They gave each other a tight, long hug before they parted ways. Rosie slowly walked home thinking about how much she loved Kindra.

The next day Rosie came home from school and started to write. She wanted to let Kindra know that she was okay.

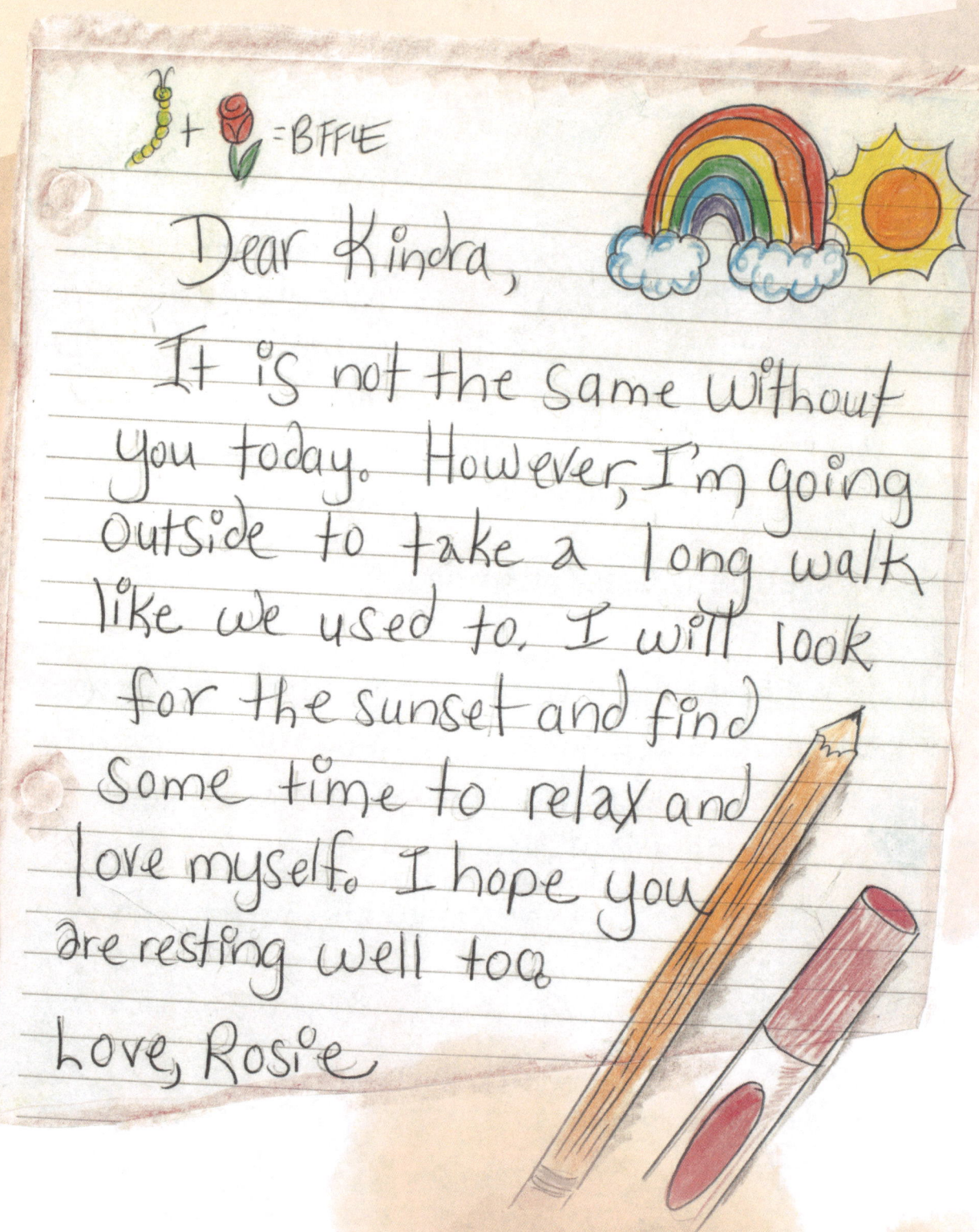

🐛 + 🌹 = BFFLE

Dear Kindra,

It is not the same without you today. However, I'm going outside to take a long walk like we used to. I will look for the sunset and find some time to relax and love myself. I hope you are resting well too.

Love, Rosie

Dear Rosie,
I am glad you are planning to spend some time outdoors. Go out and have fun! I am resting and growing. I hope to hear from you soon.

Love,
Kindra

Dear Kindra,
　It's a rainy night. I am reading a book with my new friend. She likes to read too. Her name is Grace. She has a pet cat that is so furry and soft, just like you! We are all kind to each other.
　I hope you are doing well! Good night.
　　Love,
　　Rosie

Dear Rosie,

I am so happy you found a friend. Your kindness has paid off! I'm resting a lot, but when I get out of my chrysalis, I hope I can meet your new friend. Write back soon.

Love,
Kindra

Dear Kindra, 💗❤️

I showed my friend our tree. We ran down there and took our bikes to the park. We had fun and played so many games.

Everyone worked hard in school and it was a great day!

Miss you!
Love,
Rosie ☺

Dear Rosie,

I am so happy you found friends. When you spend time with your friends, you can share your love with others. It's good to hear you are working so hard in school. It takes time and effort to learn new things. I hope to see you soon.

Love,
Kindra

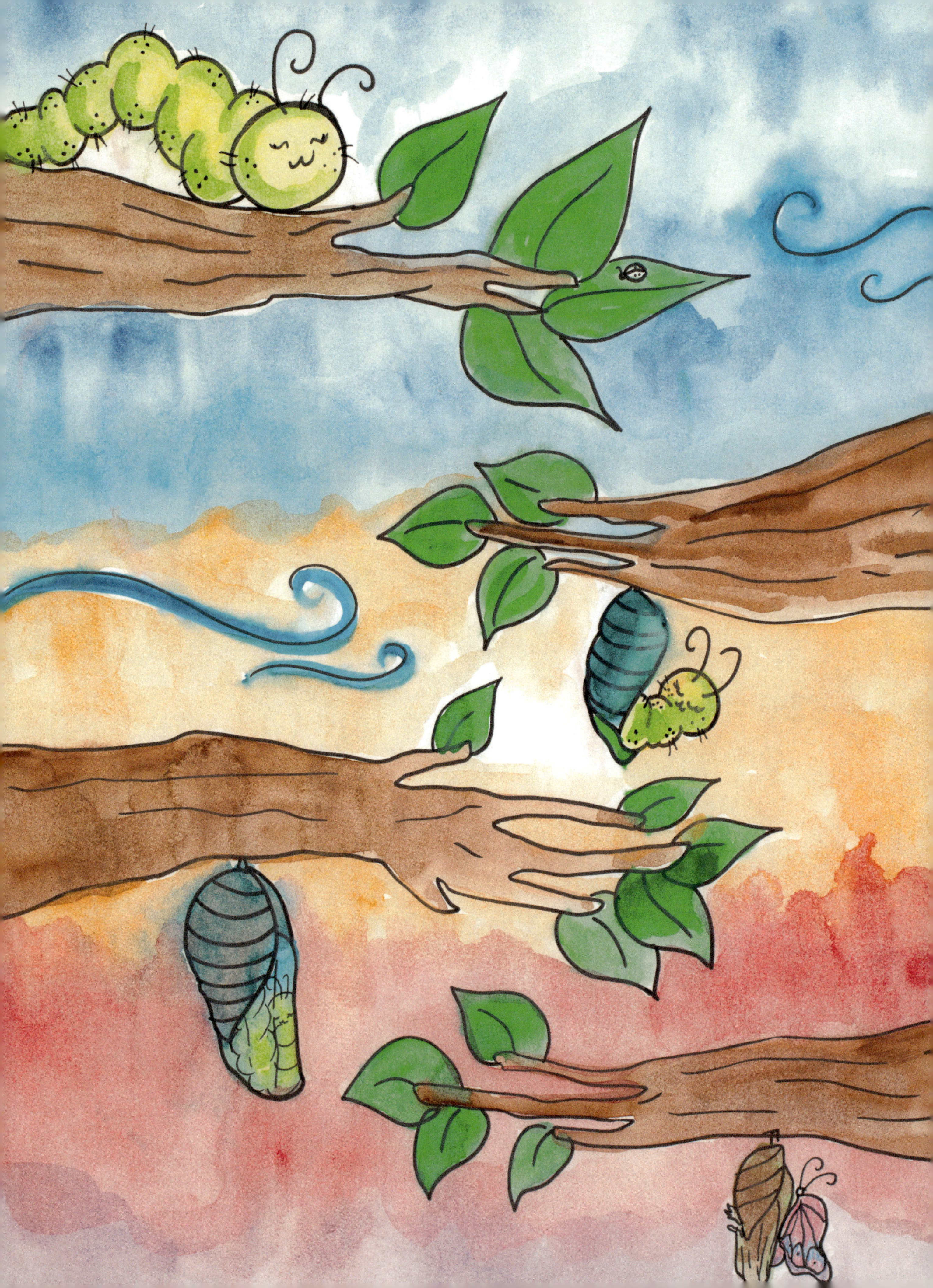

Rosie and Kindra were always excited to hear from each other. But one day, when Rosie looked into her mailbox, she didn't find a letter from Kindra.

For the next few days, Rosie ran to her mailbox, but still no letter. It was empty. She felt sad and worried about her friend.

Rosie wondered, "Is Kindra okay?"

After a few days had passed, Rosie dreamed of talking to Kindra again. She sat on her swing and thought about the special times she shared with Kindra.

Suddenly, a bright and beautiful butterfly fluttered around Rosie's head in the breeze. Rosie thought the butterfly was stunning and magnificent!

"Hi Rosie, it's me, Kindra! We can finally play together again," Kindra said, as she landed on Rosie's fingertips.

"Kindra!! Is it really you? I have missed you," said Rosie.

"Yes, it's me! You look so happy! I'm so glad I found you!" replied Kindra.

Rosie said, "You look so different. You are such an amazing, colorful, and lovely butterfly!"

"Thank you, Rosie. My rest was peaceful. I had to go through a time of transformation, just like you did," said Kindra.

"I have practiced all of the lessons you have taught me," Rosie said with a smile.

"Rosie, you have changed, too. Your smile shows that you are confident and you have learned to practice self-love. I'm so glad you found some friends and see the beauty in the world!" exclaimed Kindra.

Just like old times, Kindra and Rosie had a picnic in the park and read their favorite books.

Rosie said, "Thank you, Kindra, for your friendship. I'm so glad we are together again!"

Kindra replied, "Rosie, you are really special. You have learned that you can love yourself and find some happiness along the way."

As dusk came, Rosie and Kindra danced under the moon and the stars all through the night. When they grew tired, they fell asleep on the lush green grass.

"Kindra, where are you?"

The next morning Rosie woke up and she couldn't find Kindra anywhere. She started to call for her. Rosie sat down and noticed a piece of paper. It was another letter from Kindra!

ROSIE

Dear Rosie,

I am so proud of you, and I hope you always remember what a special person you are. I have to continue on my butterfly journey and cannot stay with you. I know that you will meet other friends and find comfort in the world around you. Remember to love yourself and share that love with others.

Love,
Kindra

Rosie thought about all the valuable lessons that Kindra had taught her. She thought, "I am enough. I can face anything and I will be fine."

As Rosie walked back home, she passed her friend Grace playing alone in her front yard.

Grace yelled, "Hey Rosie! Can you play with me?"

Rosie said, "Sure! Let's go to the top of the tree and look at some birds!"

I am enough.

Rosie and Grace climbed to the top of the tree.

Grace said, "Rosie, I have to tell you something. I am going away for a while. I have to go and visit my grandma in Europe. I might not be able to see you for a while."

Rosie said, "Oh no! I'll miss you so much, but I have an idea! We can always write letters …"

About the Author

Rene Brock is a literacy specialist who believes that stories are precious gifts that we can offer to one another. She has worked as an educator for the past thirty years, catering to students ranging from Pre-K to adults. Rene currently resides in Niagara Falls, New York and is a proud mother of two daughters, Jessica and Kristen.

Rene came up with the idea for *Letters to Kindra* with a focus on the significance of kindness and friendship in our daily lives. She arrived at the concept of *Letters From Kindra* to emphasize the importance of writing as a powerful tool for communication among people.

About the Illustrator

Lisa Pavlak is an elementary art teacher who has loved the magic of teaching art since 2009. She is grateful to her Savior, Jesus, for this opportunity and thanks her biggest supporters, her incredible husband, Mike, and her three amazing kiddos, Annabella, Max, and Bryce. She hopes to inspire the next generation of "most amazing artists" through her illustrations!

Made in the USA
Middletown, DE
14 April 2024